ADHD:
A Different Hard Drive?

By Jennie Friedman

Edited by Carolyn D'Argenio

ISBN-13: 978-1545591215
ISBN-10:1545591210

Dedication

ADHD: A Different Hard Drive? is dedicated to my dear friend, Tom Nardone. For all that we joke around about what he doesn't do, he truly is the reason you are able to read this book today, and I am grateful.

I met Tom a few years ago, one day after he reached out to me online to thank me for commenting on his story about Rudolph on his blog at tomnardone.net. His remarks were as follows:

> *"Jennie, I will be honest, I am not a coach or a therapist. I am, what I like to call...an Attention Whore. I don't even have an interest in learning about ADHD in regard to the science of it. I write funny and insightful observations and experiences that make people laugh and while I am thrilled it helps so many people, I do this primarily to get as much of the lime light as I can possibly suck up."*

We've been friends ever since and for that I am also grateful. So, bask in all your glory, Tom Nardone. You deserve it, and you are welcome.

Jennie Friedman

FOREWORD

About halfway through writing, *See in ADHD & Get Clear on What's Going On*, I realized that I was writing about three distinct things. First, there was the whole reason I began to write. After completing my education in psychology and training in ADHD coaching, I reflected on my life and the journey that brought me to now. It was extremely emotional, at times, so much so, that I'd have to set the writing aside and, sort of, "lick my wounds" so to speak. There was quite a bit about surviving my dad's suicide; yet, a memoir was not my intention. I thought so much about the nature of invisible disabilities, especially those in my own family, including chronic anxiety, major depressive disorder, bipolar disorder, ADHD, dementia, and rheumatoid arthritis. My father's struggle with severe chronic depression, ADHD, and bipolar disorder was too much for him. He committed suicide in 1987, when I was 20 years old.

In the years since his death, I have tried to make sense of what happened to him and to our family. Children of parents who commit suicide often ruminate over what they could have done differently to prevent the death. As I continue to gain clarity, I know there is nothing I can do now to heal the relationship between my father and me. I loved my father and I felt loved by him, but there were some things that I didn't understand and some things he insulated me from. I have made serious efforts to fill in the missing pieces of the puzzle and to educate myself of what was going on. I can acknowledge his suffering as very real, and I can move forward by sharing my pains, frustrations, and learning. I do this because my story is not entirely unique and I believe we must share with one another in order to heal and grow. So, yes, to those who have asked, writing is good therapy. Restoration has indeed become a byproduct of my writing.

Second, I was taking in all the information that I could find to give my book the factual foundation that is so desperately missing from many ADHD resources. But I couldn't help relating everything I was learning to personal experiences; my critical thinking skills were bursting into overdrive. In beginning my coaching career and connecting with others, the common question, "What is going on?" just kept coming to mind. I continued to look to the pioneers and professionals in the ADHD world, especially many of the ADHD coaches who have translated their life's experience into their life's work. I absorbed the lessons they taught and the discoveries they shared but I was getting frustrated with what I saw as a growing disconnect between the medical professionals who treat ADHD and the individuals who have it. Living with and loving my family and friends with ADHD helps me embrace it as a difference in cognitive function rather than pathology.

I developed a model from all of the information I had synthesized, which helps describe what is going on for a person with ADHD. As a non-ADHD person who believes that someone with this condition is as normal as I am, my hope was to better explain ADHD to other non-ADHD people like me; the ADHD co-pilots, as I like to call us. Invisible disabilities are just that, invisible. It takes a lot of faith sometimes for someone to buy into the fact that there are unseen processes at work within an individual, influencing the way they are in this world, especially among those who aren't aware of diagnostic criteria. These influences can seem mysterious and defy reason, but they are very real. They are indeed at work, holding the person with ADHD sort of hostage as much as the way you're wired controls you. The need to explain this phenomenon to others using simple language became another byproduct of my writing.

Then there was, of course, my story. The one I set out to write in the first place before going down the rabbit holes of childhood recounts and devising inspired models. My ADHD story is one of personal transformation from being someone who distanced herself from her dysfunctional family, only to eventually return, but with new insights; I could now "See in ADHD". That is what I ultimately want to share. I want to teach it, explain it, talk about it, and model it. I want anyone who is touched by ADHD to understand that this person is not willfully doing things to drive you insane. There's a lot going on, for them, for you, and for the relationship you share.

So, while I continue to work separately on my initial book, I've decided that there is no reason not to go ahead and start the sharing process by publishing the model through which I made sense out of ADHD. That is what this book is about.

As the first of my books, it helps lay the foundational framework from which one can understand ADHD, not just on a scientific level, but also on an anti-stigma level. Once I was able to "See in ADHD" my judgment disappeared. I could just get to the business of loving again. That's something I think we can all get behind as we are all in this together.

People who want a general understanding of ADHD can read this and walk away with a good idea that is helpful enough in their lives. When you begin to accept differences as the combined effect of several genes, that make each person unique, you begin to see more of what we share as humans. Apparently, there is no universal wiring of our nervous systems.

Jennie Friedman

I.

*"When **I** is replaced by **We**, illness*

becomes wellness."

~ Shannon L. Alder

Jennie Friedman

MORE THAN ONE UNDERSTANDING OF ADHD

Most people lack a proper understanding of what ADHD is and so many different explanations have been developed. The worst is ignorant prejudice spewed by those who vocalize conclusions about the people who have it. An example of this would be, "People with ADHD could control themselves if they wanted to." Other understandings are outdated beliefs such as the affected individual had *minimal brain function* or *a morbid defect of moral control*.[1] Another understanding is that there are several "types" of ADHD like the "ring-of-fire-type". This is most likely because different symptoms show up in various ways and in varying degrees of severity within the ADHD population. Basically, these "types" are just descriptions of how ADHD symptoms appear in different people. Still, others think that ADHD is a combination of different conditions, like obsessive-compulsive disorder (OCD) coupled with anxiety, and shouldn't be lumped together and called ADHD. Everyone needs to ignore all four of these strains of understanding as they are rooted in faulty logic and leave so many individuals feeling confused, broken, and sometimes hopeless.

ADHD is characterized as an invisible condition. Couple this with the lack of understanding about what its symptoms even are and it's easy to see why so many sufferers don't seek help, especially adults. It's estimated that over six percent of the adult population have ADHD and a little over half of them do not know they have the condition.[2] Invisible conditions can be challenging for scientists to study. ADHD rarely travels alone, so coexisting conditions, like learning disorders, anxiety, or depression is usually intertwined, sometimes sharing symptoms. This explains why ADHD hasn't always been addressed as a distinct condition. The unfortunate consequence of decades of misunderstanding ADHD is that it became sort of the wild west of pathologies for professionals. Many doctors and researchers have been operating on their individual hypotheses for so long without anything preventing a lot of misinformation and bad practices from spreading.

There is no known blood test or brain scan that provides definitive diagnosis at the time of this writing. Rather, there are a myriad of neuropsychological tests using old-fashioned paper-and-pencil and self-reports combined with doctor / patient interviews that determine if a person has ADHD. Unfortunately, some professionals have developed their own batteries of tests requiring thousands of dollars, which don't have peer-reviewed scientific support. When an individual chooses to go this route for diagnosis it gives them a heavily vested interest in the results, making it all too easy to dismiss what would most likely be more helpful information or treatment garnered from the traditional tests. Recently, I was discussing ADHD with a woman who smiled as she confidently informed me that she has "the 13th type of ADHD." When asked what that meant, she confessed she had no idea, but she seemed happy to slap a label on what she's been living with her whole life. I question, ultimately, how beneficial this invalid diagnosis will be.

Some professionals say natural supplements are all you need but there are numerous reports dismissing this stating there's no conclusive evidence that supplements do much of anything for people with ADHD more than what they do for people without it. Companies that sell supplements are not regulated in the same way as pharmaceutical companies meaning they don't have the same standards or research backing their claims that the pharmaceutical industry has had to provide by law for decades. I'm confident that nutrition is vital to brain health, but there's a conflict of interest when the same individuals promoting specific supplements as THE treatment for ADHD are profiting off these sales.

Some people claim that ADHD was made up by *big-pharma* to scare people into taking drugs. That doesn't even make sense. Just looking at the science we know researchers have continuously demonstrated the ability of stimulants to relieve the key symptoms of inattention, hyperactivity, and impulsivity relatively minor side effects.[3] Additionally, everyone I know, family and clients alike, all say medication has helped them with their ADHD symptoms, that is, if they have tried medication without experiencing negative side effects. The people who have had negative side effects are often too scared to try any other medication or dosage. It's understandable to be skittish, but there are a number of medications for ADHD, not including the off-label, yet effective substances, such as Phentermine, Provigil, and Nuvigil to try. It can take years to come up with the right dose of the right substance. And, as we change (hormones, for example) and as our bodies adjust to substances, changes in medication may need to be made throughout the Lifespan. Experimentation and adjustment are natural processes of treating ADHD.

So, whom should you turn to for valid, legitimate help if you suspect or have ADHD? There are many qualified doctors, but do your homework to find the doctor who is the right fit for you. Who is in your insurance plan may be important, but within or beyond those options are some things to consider. How qualified are they? Do they specialize in ADHD? Can they provide references? I suggest child psychologists/psychiatrists even for adults because ADHD is more known as a childhood condition and these professionals are more familiar with it and know that it's lifelong.

The DSM-5

The medical community relies on the *Diagnostic and Statistical Manual of Mental Disorders*, Fifth Edition (*DSM-5*) to diagnose all things mental. It is put out by the American Psychiatric Association (APA) and is used as a classification and diagnostic tool. Since its updated version, in 2013, when some changes were made regarding ADHD, there continues to be some confusion regarding its diagnosis.

Let's go over a couple of points that are important to understand. The term "on the spectrum" has many people feeling that ADHD is a part of

Autism Spectrum Disorder (ASD). It is not, although there is some brain functioning overlap of certain traits. Simply, the term "spectrum" is used to describe the broad array of symptoms and their degrees of severity, not the disorder. ADHD is a distinct condition and while it is not on the same spectrum as Autism, individuals with Autism can also have ADHD.

The DSM-5 no longer presents different "types" of ADHD. [4] By this, I mean the previous distinction made between ADD and ADHD. This reflects how our collective understanding has evolved over the years. We used to think of hyperactivity (the H in ADHD) as a symptom that not everyone shared and those who had it generally outgrew it. Now we know it simply presents differently in adults. Hyperactivity in adults shows up less outwardly as physical restlessness and more inwardly as a racy mind. The DSM-5 has given us the single designation, ADHD, for now, but it's subject to change in future editions as we continue to advance our knowledge.

The DSM-5 describes two presentations, three when combining the first two:

1. Inattention

2. Impulsivity and Hyperactivity

3. Combination of inattention, impulsivity, and hyperactivity

People can present as one or the other or as a combination and they may switch from one to the other and even back and forth between them in varying areas during their lifetime. Symptoms have three degrees of severity, mild, moderate, and severe. This depends on the extent to which the symptoms interfere with daily tasks.

The DSM-5 continues by listing traits and giving parameters for diagnosis, such as age of onset and number of environments where ADHD symptoms are causing difficulty. There are 18 symptoms from which to choose, including *"Often loses things necessary for tasks and activities"* and *"Is often 'on the go' acting as if 'driven by a motor'."* The criteria which must be met includes six or more of those symptoms within the category of either inattention or hyperactivity-impulsivity, for children up to age 16, or five or more for adolescents 17 and older and adults. These symptoms must also have been present for at least six months, and are inappropriate for the individual's developmental level. In addition, the symptoms were present before age 12, experienced in two or more different settings, interfere with normal functioning, and are not better explained by another mental disorder.[5]

Different Treatments

Unfortunately, there is no consensus about how to treat ADHD. Not all doctors agree with one another. Many view ADHD as something to fix with medication or behavioral therapy. Nutrition and sleep are also important. The most experienced experts in the field suggest a multimodal approach such as combining pharmacology, behavioral therapy, and a high protein diet. Nontraditional treatments include coaching, mindfulness training, biofeedback, elimination diets, supplements, and essential oils.

Many ADHD professionals are out to change the negativity that surrounds the ADHD diagnosis. While most doctors focus on impairment and remediation there are a few who believe it's more advantageous to focus on strengths and simply manage weaknesses. In this aspect, they've adopted what is called the *coach approach*. Coaches are the other professionals, besides doctors and clinicians, who help people with ADHD. Their focus is on just what is, meeting the individual as they are without trying to "fix" them. Coaches help individuals with ADHD devise ways in which to work around or through their challenges. My hope is that a unified singular concept will one day be universal along with standard treatment but as long as everyone in authority continues to focus on little pieces of the same whole, the understanding of ADHD will most likely continue to be fragmented.

The Shiny Tribe

Aside from medical and other healthcare professionals, teachers, coaches, and family members who deal first-hand with those who have ADHD, there are the people themselves who have it. Many of these individuals collectively consider themselves part of a "shiny tribe" who share the commonality of having ADHD, no matter their unique traits.

The word shiny is often used because it illustrates something standing out, capturing one's attention. While what that may be is unique to individuals some also use the term to describe these unique individuals. It's important to note that some others find the term "shiny" as derogatory because of the stigma attached to it. There is more about stigma in the final chapter.

Many people with ADHD believe that theirs provides them with super powers. To this point, and on the other hand, the very prominent ADHD specialist, Dr. Barkley, urges people with ADHD to not make light of their deficits. He's seen many individuals who suffer, with great difficulty, in creating and maintaining relationships and employment. He encourages the viewpoint that those with ADHD, who have accomplished great things, have done so despite their ADHD, not because of it.[6]

My father had ADHD and a lot of the coexisting conditions that often accompany it. He eventually committed suicide. So, I agree with Dr. Barkley about the serious negative impacts ADHD can have on someone. Yet, I am more concerned about the way many of the professionals solely rely on our increasingly outdated medical model of healthcare, where ADHD is seen as pathology, making those with it, in need of fixing. Such a model implies that the people with ADHD are broken, a concept that continues to debilitate individuals and their families. This stigma must end.

I have been surrounded by ADHD throughout my life, personally and professionally. I know first-hand how many misunderstandings and miscommunication can happen in a relationship between someone with ADHD and someone without it. Some of these disconnects have had heart-wrenching results. It doesn't have to be this way. By learning to see in ADHD it gets better because you are able to see through the other's eyes.

Jennie Friedman

II.

"This stuff isn't rocket science."

~ Mike Tadych

Jennie Friedman

UNDERSTANDING OUR EXECUTIVE FUNCTIONS

Dr. Thomas E. Brown, Ph.D., Dr. Russell Barkley, Ph.D., and Dr. William W. Dodson, M.D. are recognized experts in the field of ADHD. In my studies I saw both Dr. Brown and Dr. Barkley's work referenced most often and so the magnitude of their contributions cannot be overstated. Dr. Brown is a clinical psychologist. He received his Ph.D. from Yale University and has published numerous papers and books detailing his research on ADHD.[7] Dr. Barkley has presented worldwide, received several prestigious awards in clinical psychology and neuropsychology, and has published over 200 articles and book chapters related to ADHD and its coexisting conditions.[8] Their bodies of work combined have helped form our modern understanding. Dr. Dodson is a board-certified psychiatrist who has specialized in adults with ADHD for the last 23 years.[9] He has a thriving practice and contributes regularly to *ADDitude Magazine*. As authorities in the field each has devoted their career to exploring the brain as it relates to ADHD.

Dr. Brown developed the theory of human executive functions to help describe the subconscious processes that are impaired in people with ADHD.[10] Since this is key in my work, I have devoted this chapter detailing his model of the executive functions. His efforts are fundamental in what has quickly become an accepted mainstream understanding of ADHD. They are what Dr. Barkley refers to when he describes ADHD as "an executive function dysfunction". Drawing from his medical background, Dr. Dodson looked for a shared feature by everyone with ADHD that is absent in people who are non-ADHD; thus, developing his theory that the nervous system is wired differently in people with ADHD than those without it.[11] He puts forth that the ADHD nervous system has its own set of rules. My work was influenced by all three of these ADHD specialists and thought leaders.

I used Dr. Brown and Dr. Barkley's ideas around executive functions and Dr. Dodson's ideas around the nervous system and created a different model of understanding ADHD. The link between the executive function and the nervous system is that the former is a function of the latter and the nervous system operates subconsciously. This means the executive function is dependent on subconscious processes.[12] This set the stage for my hypothesis: when the executive function seems impaired because it is not performing typically, it is performing atypically, and in that, it isn't impaired, it's just operating differently. I agree with Dr. Dodson that the "secret" to ADHD lies in the human nervous system and think more research in this direction will guide our future understanding.[13] The model I've designed is the topic of this book and focuses on the subconscious influences we do see in individuals with ADHD, not the ones we don't or are considered impaired.

Making sense of the neuroscience is essential in laying a foundation from which to understand ADHD; yet, I am not a doctor and don't pretend to be. I'm an ADHD coach. Many of the people I work with have expressed a disdain for science but want to know what's going on with either themselves or their loved ones who have ADHD. I want to use simple language so that people like them don't feel they're getting a science lesson as much as just hearing what ADHD is all about. So, the simple definition of ADHD that we'll use is: "… a developmental impairment of the brain's self-management system, the executive functions."[14]

There are many sections in our brains. The section that ADHD affects most is in the pre-frontal cortex (PFC). This is the area that controls our executive functions. Now realize, the executive function is not an actual physical thing, like a vein or an eardrum, it's a construct explaining specific activities which occur subconsciously within the brain. Dr. Brown likens the role of the executive function system to that of an orchestra conductor. Consider the way a conductor manages which instruments play when. The executive functions manage the ways certain subconscious brain activities, such as organizing, operate. It's our brain management system's manager (sort of like your boss' boss.) Just as when the conductor is unavailable or directs the wrong instruments to play at the wrong time, the result is less than harmonious (though every now and then the result can be a beautiful, unexpected melody). The executive function activities are meant to work together in a future-oriented way. When the system isn't running properly, instruments don't play at the right time or along with the right counterpart. That's what can happen with ADHD. Certain brain activities don't always work together or in various combinations harmoniously.

Dr. Brown's model describes the executive function's six clusters of activity: activation, focus, effort, emotion, memory, and action. It also details what subconscious processes make up each cluster. This book details the first three. For many people ADHD does not significantly affect every cluster, nor does it affect each cluster the same way. The combinations are endless. According to Eric Tivers, host of the ADHD reWired Podcast; there are 86,000 various combinations of ADHD traits, all of which vary in degree of severity and combination.[15] Even if neuroscience doesn't fascinate you, you have to admit, that's amazing. At the very least, we can begin to understand why it's been so difficult to figure out exactly what ADHD is and what's causing it.

ACTIVATION

Activation includes getting started on something, like work, but that's not all. There's more to getting started than simply getting started. Organizing what we are doing, like making scrambled eggs, and with what we need to do it, like getting the eggs, the frying pan, and spatula are all included. Estimating time and being able to prioritize what must get done, in what order, are also involved. This explains why procrastination is one of the symptoms of ADHD directly related to activation. From the non-ADHD perspective, the person is putting off things, even very important things, until a sense of urgency becomes strong enough to finally motivate them. The person with ADHD may come off as irresponsible or uncaring and it can be frustrating. It's as if the concept of importance does not exist, and, in fact, for them it doesn't in the same way as someone without ADHD. Those with ADHD also often have a different sense of time. They don't feel time passing like non-ADHD people do.

FOCUS

Focusing, sustaining focus, and shifting focus for tasks, are all included in the cluster of FOCUS. This area addresses attention. (In this chapter, focus and attention are used interchangeably.) People with ADHD will tell you they don't have a deficit of attention; they have too much attention; indeed that is the case. Their attention is divided, given to this, to that, and to everything else, and that comes off as distractibility. ADHD is seen as an inability to regulate external stimuli. For example, in a classroom, a teacher may be up at the board writing a math problem. While the student with ADHD notices this, he or she also notices the kid at the next desk tapping their shoe lightly, and the lawnmower whirring off in the distance, and the clock ticking and the person with loud shoes walking down the hall, and the weird way the pencil is writing. With their executive function not optimally filtering, competing stimuli doesn't get automatically, subconsciously, sorted through and prioritized. Everything comes at them with the same intensity! The child must consciously decide what to focus on and that, by the way, can be exhausting.

EFFORT

The activities within the cluster of EFFORT include regulating alertness, sustaining effort, and processing speed. Many with ADHD make what we call "great sprinters;" they can perform amazingly well at short-term projects but often lose steam and may well never finish something they have started. The level of interest an individual has for what they are doing is usually the determining factor for how much effort they'll exert. This ties the clusters of EFFORT and ACTIVATION together. Problems in effort can also be seen in sleep behaviors such as not getting to sleep on time, staying up too late, and not being able to easily become alert in the morning.

Many ADHD professionals refer to Dr. Brown's Model of ADHD because it clearly illustrates ADHD's impact on the six clusters of brain activities the subconscious processes in each. This book covers the first three clusters of activity:

Cluster of Activity   Subconscious Processes

1. ACTIVATION   organizing, prioritizing, activating to work

2. FOCUS   focusing, sustaining and shifting attention

3. EFFORT   regulating alertness, sustaining effort, and processing speed

III.

"ADHD: A Different Hard Drive."

~ Jennie Friedman

Jennie Friedman

ADHD: A DIFFERENT HARD DRIVE?

Dr. Brown's ADHD Model presents what's being impaired in the executive function. Because it provides such a great description of which activities the executive function system manages, we are going to use it as the foundation for an even deeper understanding. Though instead of looking at what the ADHD brain is not doing; we're going to focus on what it is doing! Using Dr. Brown's findings we can assume the executive function is regulating certain clusters of activities. The question now is: what is influencing how the brain does this? It is the subconscious programs (neural networks) that are responsible for automatic responses.[16] These subliminal drivers, which influence the activities in each cluster, are part of our nervous system.[17] Understanding their influence provides a clearer understanding of the unique way people with ADHD are "wired."

What the ADHD Brain IS Doing

Following is a model to help visually demonstrate how ADHD really is like a different hard drive. In the squares underneath each circle, are the activities listed from within each of Dr. Brown's six clusters of activities of the executive function. The subconscious processes - the primary influencers fueling activities - are seen in the circles; they are the drivers of each activity. You can see that usually what influences the non-ADHD brain is quite different from what influences the ADHD brain.

These invisible influences are layered in the subconscious, operating beneath our awareness. For example, when I walk into my kitchen and intend to clean it, within milliseconds, my subconscious mind has set objectives into action. My mind isn't computing the how and what to do; it's sensing patterns, which become the drivers, and I respond appropriately.[18] My mind considers time, importance, sequence, and order. It's as if it automatically "knows" where to start, how to start, what to do, and what the outcome will look like. Simply put, ADHD stems from having a uniquely designed nervous system. A person with ADHD doesn't experience cleaning the kitchen like I do. Their subconscious automatically considers interest, challenge, curiosity, and urgency instead.[19] This may cause the person with ADHD to look at the messy kitchen, see the one thing that interests them, grab that, and turn around and leave.

As a society, one challenge is to stop thinking that because a person with ADHD doesn't automatically consider time, importance, sequence, and order when they clean their kitchen, that they are then somehow incompetent or lazy. Later examples look at some of the consequences of not "thinking" in the same way as a non-ADHD person, but the point is, someone with ADHD is often challenged by the routines and boring tasks of daily life. They aren't defective, though it forces them to operate differently. Maybe ADHD should stand for *A Different Hard Drive*.

IV.

"Organizing is much better than cleaning."

~ Alejandra Costello

Jennie Friedman

ORGANIZING, PRIORITIZING, ACTIVATING & TIME ESTIMATION

In ACTIVATION, the non-ADHD brain subconsciously is considering initiating actions, planning, and strategizing. It's also subconsciously processing sequences and order, "should this be done in terms of beginning, middle, and end, or should it be alphabetized?" [20] Similarly, it considers the past, present, and future. Time estimation uses an inner sense of time and priorities are based on importance.

ACTIVATION in a NON-ADHD BRAIN

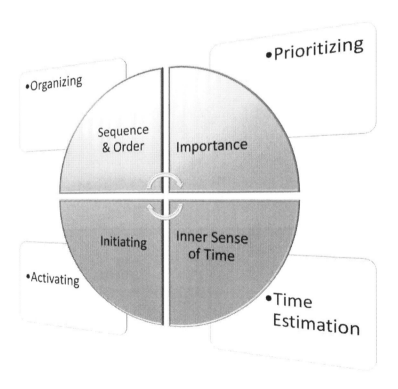

ACTIVATION in an ADHD BRAIN

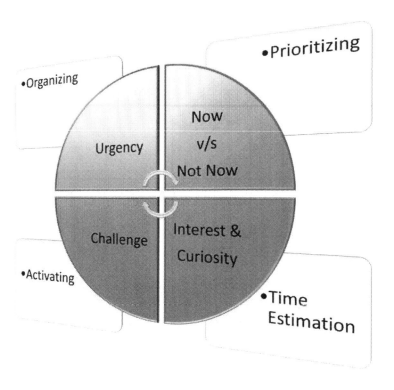

Here, interest, curiosity, and challenge are being considered to create organizational structure rather than sequencing and order. Now, it's easy to see how someone with ADHD jumps into the middle of a messy room and doesn't know where to start in order to clean it. This is also why, so often, they will find something in the mess and get distracted, forgetting to clean altogether. *Now vs. Not Now* is also factored into the activities and subconsciously, it's considering only what's interesting, is curious about, or knows is urgent.[21]

The Big O of ADHD

Organization could be considered the "Big O" of ADHD. Not because it feels good but because it's one of the biggest challenges of ADHD affecting task completion and even communication. A huge revelation for me came from learning that a person with ADHD does not think in terms of a beginning, middle, and end, a process of the executive function within the cluster of ACTIVATION. Just imagine how chaotic any activity, which consists of more than several components, can seem, if you only view it as a whole and cannot ascertain or order steps? Probably nothing demonstrates this point more than the subject of housecleaning does.

Cleaning is one of those activities that can utterly bring an otherwise motivated busy individual to a complete standstill. I become completely paralyzed when tasked with the demonic chore of cleaning my house and I know I cannot for the life of me defend that. It just is. I know that not liking to clean is not unique to ADHD and I realize there are some people with ADHD who are ultra clean. But for most people with ADHD, clutter is an issue. As an ADHD coach, this has been discussed with many clients and the consensus is because cleaning is SO insanely boring.

Let's see...there's showroom clean, medium clean, messy, and then there's the *HOT MESS*. Yes, maybe it sounds insulting, but it's more fun to say than just very messy. I know several hot messy people. They border on hoarder. There's no cleaning the dishes every night, no mopping floors, no dusting. None. I know one woman with ADHD who pays a maid service to come in about twice a year with bulldozers to clean up after her family's tsunami. Other than not cleaning though, she's a devoted mother of four who is non-stop busy. She's running one of the four somewhere every day after school, and she's a brilliant schoolteacher, making a great salary, working responsibly daily during the school year and being the fun mom all summer.

Someone with ADHD does not think in a linear fashion, so many traditional ways of organizing fly out the window and are replaced with unique systems. For example, take how a non-ADHD person may handle their incoming mail and where they put their keys. There is often one place for each, a spot on an office desk for the mail and a hook by the door for the keys. I even know one very messy non-ADHD person who will keep her mail on a chair in the living room and her keys by the phone in the den. The point is that there is a home for each and rarely is there a deviation from their designated areas.

Because people with ADHD have different drivers influencing ACTIVATION and MEMORY, they may not think of things as having "homes". Mail comes in and lands where it lands, not to be seen again unless being hunted for at a later date or stumbled across while looking for something else. Keys too, are dropped when they are no longer needed. Some make it into bathrooms, others get set down in bedrooms and covered up with clothing, and still others stay in the keyhole of the front door, not to be found until one leaves the house to go look for them in the car. Yeah, some are left in the car, but only if someone else is in house or the entrance was originally unlocked.

The curve-linear world of ADHD has only the NOW, not a past, present, and future...not a beginning, middle, and end. This is seen in many activities like cleaning the house, for example. Because they don't see a beginning, they will usually just jump in and start somewhere, sort of working in all directions simultaneously. Traditional organization becomes unsustainable because it requires a sense of linearity, importance, and time. If your brain doesn't automatically consider these three things, then no wonder the house is a mess. How could it not be, right?

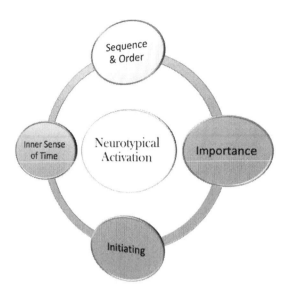

This is what we mean by the ADHD brain being uniquely wired.

Wrong. Actually, when house cleaning is either an engaging challenge or somehow interesting, it can and does get done, sometimes exceptionally well. One of my friends with ADHD, in particular, keeps her home impeccably tidy. She especially keeps her living room and kitchen spotless. She doesn't keep track of her keys, but it's never because they get lost in a mess. This just goes to show you, ADHD is as unique to individuals as individuals are to one another.

Black-and-White Thinking

Viewing things as a whole and being unable to ascertain or order steps also accounts for a person's black-and-white thinking. For many people with ADHD, everything can seem like all-or-nothing situations. As an example, when I told my friends with ADHD about writing this series, each one suggested not to worry about a title or how to structure chapters, just write and let the creativity flow. "Don't get stuck trying to break everything down," one advised. Conversely, each of my friends without ADHD asked me what the title was, knowing I had not yet begun the writing process. Most of them advised me to write an outline first so that the structure of the book would come easily. Wow! This isn't just a difference in thinking it's a difference in approach.

It's hard for me to imagine approaching everything in life without sort of breaking it down first because that's how I'm wired. It makes total sense that if your subconscious isn't doing this for you, then it would seem like a chore. No wonder situations that call for this are more difficult and time consuming for someone with ADHD. Examples of these situations include packing for trips, grocery shopping, writing papers, paying bills, paying taxes, doing laundry, writing expense reports, or any other itemized report, scheduling, buying gifts, keeping track of car maintenance, and so on.

Probably one of the most commonly known symptoms of ADHD is being chronically late to everything. I'm not saying people with ADHD are always late to every place they have to go but many are often late enough to create undue hardship on themselves and others. One reason for this is that their perception of time is different from those without ADHD. It can appear as though they are not paying attention to the clock or just don't care. This was my thought originally, but the truth is that it's just not that cut-and-dry.

Be Realistic About How Long it Takes to Do Something

This is strange advice, isn't it? I mean, who sets out to be unrealistic? Just imagine hearing, "Honey, I'm going for groceries, I'll be back in 4 hours." Wouldn't you wonder, "How much food do we need?" But, if you have ADHD this really happens all the time, and there's no abundance of groceries showing up at the door. So how exactly does a 45-minute trip to the store end up taking hours? Well, for starters, it probably depends on the store. If it's one of the big-box sorts, there were probably lots of interesting items that triggered many imaginative explorations into endless possibilities, which equal having had to make decisions, and THAT takes time. In fact, a whole inner-conversation can take minutes and that's just with one item! Now imagine what happens if there's a long grocery list. What if the grocery store is only one of two or three stops? Stores are full of colorful displays competing for the buyers' attentions. Plus, there are other people there…people to talk to, look at, and maneuver around.

Now vs. Not Now

Rather than having an internal clock, which perceives the passing of time, people with ADHD experience time from two sorts of "time zones" - commonly referred to as *Now* and *Not Now*. For instance, if something is not happening *Now* then it's happening *Not Now;* things that are *Not Now* do not need to be attended to. That is why you'll see an individual with ADHD perform, what seems as, quite well, under pressure. For example, the project they've had months to work on was due *Not Now* until maybe just a day or two before *Now*. To people without ADHD this can seem mystifying and maddening. It can also negatively impact many areas of life: career, intimate relationships, family, and others' perceptions of them.

This *Now vs. Not Now* orientation can be very frustrating for both the individuals with ADHD and those without it. I've worked with many clients who think they can do "just one more thing" because they have no frame of reference on how long things take to do. The result is they are late for appointments or responsibilities even ones as important as work. One woman I know is continuously late to pick up her son from school, even though dismissal happens at the exact same time every day. Perhaps inexcusable, but this is the mother's ADHD in action.

What are the repercussions the mother may experience? For one, her son may not feel as secure with his mother as he could. Also, the staff at the school may view the mom in a negative light. She comes off as extremely busy at best and irresponsible at worst. A person with ADHD comes by this honestly; really, they can't help it, without creating systems and supports to externalize this function. Their brains are simply wired differently. So, although, intellectually this woman knows she must go get her son, she will look at the clock. "Ok, I have twenty-five minutes until I need to be there," she'll think. Now, this next thought is not coming from her conscious mind, but her brain registers, "Hmm, that's *Not Now* "and she will proceed to do something else like put a load of laundry in the washer. Then she'll look back at the clock and she is supposed to be there in five minutes. "Ok, *Now*" comes another subconscious command. She leaves her house and the drive takes fifteen minutes. She then arrives at the school; she is ten minutes late…again.

The fascinating thing about this scenario is there many components simultaneously at work here. For one, she is not sensing the passage of time in the non-ADHD way. Next, she is feeling the need to fill up empty space, (the time those without ADHD use to transition from one task to another) with a completely new activity like loading the washer, not at all aware that this will cause her to be late. This is because her brain's wiring is not automatically considering how long it takes to do things. She also isn't wired to think back to when she loaded the washer to estimate how long it would take. (See EFFORT)

Her brain may also be responding to an unintended consequence of waiting until the last minute. She could experience a dopamine boost in the brain by the rush to get there as she surely sees by the time she is driving that she must now hurry. These energy bursts feel really good to the ADHD brain. In fact, people with ADHD need them in order to activate the part of the executive function that non-ADHD people have activated for them subconsciously, no matter the activity. This brings up yet another element. The person with ADHD may find routine tasks so mundane that their brain never trips the ACTIVATION signal whereas someone with a non-ADHD brain does not require any extra stimulation to do even the most soul-crushingly boring tasks. That's not to say they are done with great pleasure, but non-ADHD brains can activate seemingly independent of interest while ADHD brains do not as easily.

Dopamine, Please

What can provide this extra stimulation? Caffeine or particular stimulant medications can usually do the trick, but not for all people in all cases. Just as the ADHD brain is different from the non-ADHD brain, so too are ADHD brains different from one another. Some respond better to neuronal reuptake inhibitors, non-stimulant drugs, and others still do not respond well to any medication. The natural way to provide this needed stimulation is to engage the brain in areas of strength and interest or tap into curiosity. While this is true for everyone, it is especially true for those with ADHD.

When people with ADHD are engaged in activities they either really love or are extremely curious about, you may not see symptoms of ADHD. Have you always gone by the "Do the hardest thing first to get it out of the way" strategy? For people with ADHD, this is a horrible strategy. Having them engage in something they love first will provide them a natural dopamine boost, sometimes just enough to provide that oomph they need to get started on a more difficult task next. This is why kids might do awesome in some subjects but awful in others.

Now is as good a time as any to talk about a common activity, which stimulates all brains, video games. There's a difference though for people with ADHD, and it has to do with them not having the same inner reward system as those without ADHD. Video games provide instant gratification, which, in turn, gives instant dopamine boosts. Instant reward is key here. People with ADHD have a harder time engaging in an activity when the payoff is in the future. Remember, they don't really sense the future like a non-ADHD person. So, you can see how all areas affected by ADHD sort of inter-relate with one another.

Lastly, I want to add that although time insensitivity can be an obvious challenge, when framed in a strengths perspective, this same person could be seen as having an internal organization that's unique to them, affording them a certain mystique in a positive way. Remember the mother chronically late to pick up her son? This same woman is also somewhat of socialite in certain affluent circles and is viewed within them as always being "fashionably late". In this context, her tardiness works in her favor. People may be curious, "What important thing was she doing before she got here?" Rather than be constrained by structured time she feels she lives in an intuitive flow. Individuals like her can be highly productive in areas of strengths and interests and quite creative and successful when they shore up some supports around their weaknesses.

Prioritizing

Another consequence of having a *Now vs. Not Now* mentality is that it also affects the ability to set priorities. Thoughts of planning and delegating don't occur naturally in the ADHD brain, mostly because what registers as important depends on what is interesting or has an approaching deadline. If it is boring, forget it, it's unimportant. Take the example of housecleaning again. I hate to keep bringing it up, but it really drives home the point. Few people are interested in doing housecleaning but do it because it's important. What that means to the non-ADHD person is that for a whole bunch of reasons, like maintaining a healthy environment, having order and organization, and feeling comfortable have been determined as important, even if there is no interest in doing it.

For the non-ADHD person, their regulatory system subconsciously handles a lot of decision making for them automatically. They don't have to manually set the wheels in motion, working to override the ADHD system's natural instinct to just notice what is interesting to them. The person with ADHD does not have importance influencing them. They can intellectually know that the house should be cleaned, that mail and such should be organized, dishes washed, shelves dusted, floors mopped and vacuumed, but none of that is interesting and because it is not interesting to them their brain doesn't identify it as something to engage in. They know it's important but knowing doesn't ignite them. In this, we can begin to understand how shame develops at a very early age. Shame comes from knowing that what you are "supposed" to do is different from what you do.

Now, one trick that sort of circumvents this hardwiring is to manufacture interest when there is none. We see this a lot with children in school and star charts. A kid with ADHD may have no interest in sitting still through a math lesson listening to the teacher drone on, even if they are very good at math. Tell that child that if they sit quietly and do their best to pay attention and not disrupt the class they will get to pick something out of the prize bucket or earn a star, and they can sit very still and do a great job. (That is, if they are interested in getting that reward). It is called keeping things shiny. The ADHD brain loves shiny; that is, anything interesting to them is sparkly and capture's their attention.

People with ADHD must creatively come up with new (shiny) ideas about how to engage in the things they want to do. It's in that creative process that the brain's wiring makes new and strong connections that help compensate for any weaknesses in executive function. As an example, when activities become a habit, usually after 90-120 days of consistency, the brain does access a sort of autopilot not dependent on executive function.[22] What great news! But as a loved one, try and remember the ideas really need to come from them. Hearing it from you eliminates the creative process necessary to create any lasting changes in behavior; and no one likes being told what to do anyway!

Jennie Friedman

V.

"I am not absentminded. It is the presence of mind that makes me unaware of everything else."

~ G. K. Chesterton

Jennie Friedman

FOCUSING, TRANSITIONING, SUSTAINING FOCUS & ATTENTION

Within FOCUS, the non-ADHD brain subconsciously is creating awareness through the senses and sorting through the stimuli. In this sorting process it is prioritizing, filtering out what is not important to pay attention to, from what is.[23] It can easily shift focus by considering changes in priority and it can sustain focus through willpower. This commitment is not dependent on interest, so the average person can barrel through even the most soul-crushingly boring tasks.

FOCUS in a NON-ADHD BRAIN

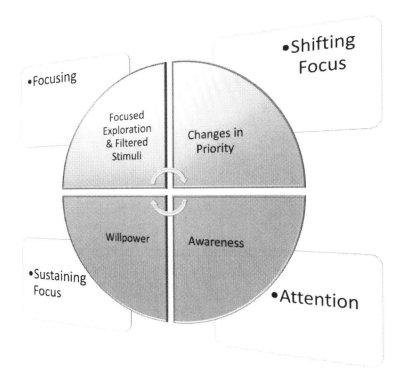

FOCUS in an ADHD BRAIN

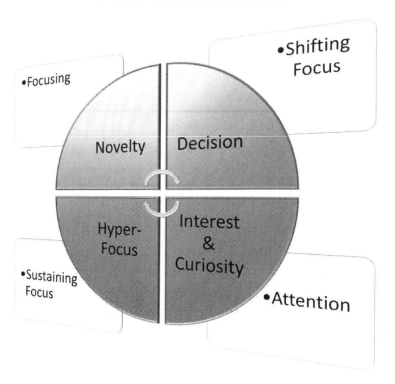

FOCUS within the ADHD brain is influenced subconsciously by interest, curiosity and novelty.[24] When there are no filters sorting through what should be ignored, only what's *shiny* (interesting) stands out. Additionally, the brain cannot easily shift focus without stopping and starting from zero again.[25] Decisions are consciously made instead of automatically, which takes an enormous amount of effort. Also, the ADHD brain cannot sustain focus through willpower; instead, it is influenced by interest. Hyper-focus can occur. This is when the brain automatically takes over the mind because it is satisfyingly engaged. Once in hyper-focus almost nothing can distract the person. A common example is when the individual gets sucked into playing video games for hours.

As we discussed earlier, many challenges for people with ADHD stem from a the fact that just about all stimuli can appear equal to the ADHD mind making it difficult to figure out what to pay attention to.[26] Again, one activity of the executive function is to filter out stimuli, which are unimportant, from stimuli, which are relevant in the moment. When everything carries with it equal weight in importance prioritizing becomes near impossible. Also, the ADHD brain's default system is set to interest. If interest and curiosity are not present it is extra hard for someone with ADHD to engage, which sadly comes off as not paying attention or not caring.

Some people with ADHD often feel they are highly sensitive or oversensitive when in fact they just don't have highly optimal functioning filters. For some, sounds are as tangible as things. I must confess this really blows my mind. It also has me rethinking about what I get frustrated with when communicating with anyone with ADHD. This filtering process is done subconsciously, automatically, in non-ADHD people. So how do people with ADHD filter when it's not automatic?

Manual Filtering

People with ADHD do have noticeably different ways of attending than do non-ADHD people. To some who do not understand ADHD, it may seem that someone who presents primarily as inattentive, especially, "loses" attention. But if you really take a moment you can see that it's not about shutting down. They are paying attention to something just not what you want them to. It could be to the thoughts bouncing in their head. Most people with ADHD will tell you they have an abundance of attention, other things become just SO interesting...and that comes off as distractibility.

Imagine walking towards the post office with only five minutes left before it closes. You must mail out a package for your boss, but your brain gets distracted as a car passes by... your mind floods with thoughts of that car, how you just saw it in the coolest commercial, other things you've seen on TV, and what should you make for dinner? You next realize you've walked twenty yards past the post office, and yup, now there's a 'Closed' sign dangling in the window.

Medication for Focus

Remember earlier we touched on how ADHD medication is effective in the area of FOCUS? I'm seeing a client now whose focus is intense on hockey. He plays whenever he can and gives lessons on a substitute basis. Unfortunately, as much as he loves the game and needs the money, he is always late when he has a class. The problem, he says, is that he is always focused on something else at the time he should be getting ready to leave the house. So, here is an example of someone extremely interested in hockey, but that doesn't seem to help in being timely. He's even been let go before because of his tardiness, so he knows what that feels like, and yet it's still not enough to modify his behavior. So far, he has tried alarms, and reminder notes, but feels like he might finally try medication as all else has failed.

Previously, I was working with a man who was almost 60 years old. He had just been diagnosed and wanted to start coaching. He told me his doctor gave him a prescription; he had it filled and took the first pill right before he went on a motorcycle ride with a group of friends. "I always go riding with the same group of guys, have for years. I just love riding my bike. I love the wind whipping against my face and the feeling of speed, I can ride for hours!" He went on to share with me that after he took his ADHD medication that first day, it took about twenty minutes, and suddenly, he said he noticed he was noticing everything! He realized that there were beautiful flowers on the side of the road; they had gorgeous colors and incredible smells. He could feel the sun warming his face, in a way he never, in almost 60 years, ever noticed. He was amazed, he said, to realize, right then and there, just how much he'd been missing his entire life because he hadn't been able to focus on anything.

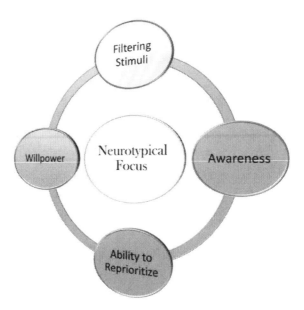

Each brain's subconscious influence is different from the others.

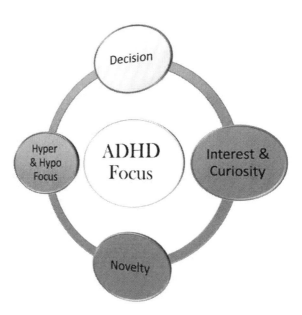

Medication and focus go hand-in-hand but it's a choice. As you see from these two men, one is considering it, but only after other non-medicinal options, and another who wishes he had found it earlier in life. I now understand that focus is something one with ADHD must do consciously, and that usually takes so much effort. Choosing how to manage successfully focusing, when you need to be focused, is a personal decision. I also have had clients share how they're afraid of not feeling like their natural selves and I respect that. There is a level of responsibility one has to choose for themselves and for their family. When it comes to ADHD, it rarely travels alone, so it can't be stressed enough how important it is to work WITH your doctor, especially considering medication options and decisions.

Jennie Friedman

VI.

"The hardest part is getting started."

~ K. C. Sherwood

Jennie Friedman

ALERTNESS, EFFORT, PROCESSING SPEED & MOTIVATION

EFFORT in a NON-ADHD BRAIN

Within EFFORT, the non-ADHD brain subconsciously utilizes benefits of regular sleep patterns including regulation of the circadian system (responsible for sleep/wake cycles). The concepts of importance (they feel it should get done) and secondary importance (when motivated by the fact someone they respect thinks the task is important) along with an internal reward system that considers rewards and consequences/punishments all influence effort.[27] Subliminally, associative areas of the brain are activated. Once

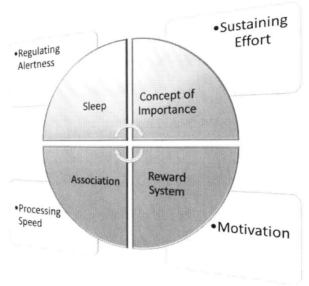

sensory information has entered, it's combined, evaluated, and compared to prior experiences, providing accurate pictures from which to operate. The association areas also process and develop plans of action and work to create out thoughts, plans, and personality.[28]

EFFORT in an ADHD BRAIN

ADHD brains also require restorative sleep but affected persons find it hard to fall asleep and stay asleep. Sleep patterns get interrupted easily, which may be due to a uniquely wired circadian system.[29] Motivation is not driven by subliminally conceptualizing importance, secondary importance, or an internal reward system but rather the person's interest and curiosity. Consequently, motivating someone with ADHD can be a challenge and explains why they can appear selfish or selfserving.[30] The ADHD brain must consciously make associations because this isn't happening on a subconscious

level. They are not automatically combining, evaluating, and comparing things to prior experiences skewing the pictures from which they process and develop plans of action. The ADHD brain's chemistry contributes to challenges in this area, specifically, dopamine levels.

Brain Chemistry

You may wonder why, if these activities are subconsciously influenced, do some doctors prescribe medication for ADHD? It's because of brain chemistry. Some of the activities regulated by the executive function are directly affected chemically as well as subliminally, primarily by two neurotransmitters: dopamine and serotonin. Dopamine affects FOCUS and EFFORT while serotonin affects EMOTION and ACTIVATION, as seen in mood, pain perception, and the sleep/wake cycle. This cycle consists of two internal influences: sleep homeostasis and circadian rhythms.[31] In essence, while all of the clusters of activities involved in executive functions are part of the nervous system and have chemical components to them, medication doesn't help every symptom of ADHD.

Since I'm a coach I cannot go into the whole area of medication with the expertise it requires but do not mistake my light touch on medication as my making light of its use. It's often part of the treatment plan for well-managed ADHD, especially in folks that show severity of symptoms. Without going into a full-blown lecture on how medication works, suffice it to say that stimulant medications are by far the most commonly used and considered the most effective. Many people benefit by having their dopamine levels raised via stimulant medication. Contrary to popular belief, stimulant medication is not stimulating physical activity, it's stimulating dopamine production.[32] There are several types of stimulant medications and they, as with all medication options, need to be discussed with your doctor.

Medication isn't a fix-all strategy though. While it does help with focus, effort, mood, and hyperactivity, it doesn't change all neural drivers, which influence activities like organizing and planning. It can't help with self-awareness or black and-white thinking either. This is why family and friends continue misunderstanding why the person with ADHD is still doing what they are doing, even after a diagnosis, or medication. It doesn't change who they are or how their nervous system is wired.

I encourage rooting your understanding of ADHD in science, if only this little bit. It's not character flaws, you see; it's **A D**ifferent **H**ard **D**rive. When it's understood that people with ADHD are doing things in such a way primarily because their brains operate with different drivers, it can really help get rid of stigma and judgment. People cannot help how they are wired. As with non-ADHD people, their nervous system operates subconsciously to influence their brains' executive functions. There is no choice in the matter; it's their biology.

Most people have inherited their ADHD traits. ADHD symptoms vary among people and within individuals over time. The effect of symptoms can range from mild, slight tendencies to severe, full-blown symptoms, or anywhere in between. ADHD does not define people. They are people with hearts and souls and deserve respect, kindness, and accommodations. They are whole, creative, and resourceful, and most, when left to their own devices, do compensate, thrive, and flourish.

Motivation

Wouldn't we all love our motivation to be externalized? Then all of that digging deep, pulling us up by the bootstrap stuff could be gone. It's a lot of work, getting motivated, especially to do things we don't want to do but have to. Obviously, depending on the individual this list could get really long. If you have ADHD, this list could be really, really long. Do you know why? One word: *interest*.

Yeah, it's really not so scientific sounding, but in general, we all feel unmotivated to do things we find boring. For people with ADHD this is even more so. Their brains are hard-wired for stimulating, shiny, sparkly things; aka, whatever interests them. The myth is that this has to be some fast and furious activity, but it's really more about getting an immediate reward.

I have a friend with ADHD who finds knitting very stimulating. She gets bored watching movies so she brings her knitting bag to the theater with her to keep her busy and better able to focus on the movie. Other friends of mine have a daughter with ADHD who runs around with boundless energy and truly, she doesn't sit still for much and never has. Yet, she loves fishing, and every summer, ever since she was really little, she could stand on the shore and fish for hours. No exaggeration. *Hours!* How could that be? Interest. She's really motivated to catch a fish, and knows she has to be very quiet and still or they won't bite. That's devotion. That's also the impact interest has on ADHD.

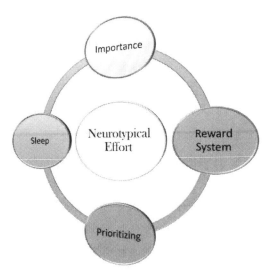

Each brain's subconscious influence is different from the others.

Just as something being important is key in motivating someone without ADHD, interest is key in motivating someone with it.

Now, let's look back at the science again. ADHD is characterized by functional impairment of regulation and inhibition.[33] Those with ADHD are less inhibited, their brain doesn't capture the *"have to do this"* signal. It's like *"have to"* reads differently. They know intellectually they have to do something, but their regulatory system isn't kicking them in the butt to do it; their priorities aren't set to importance; they are set to interest. The bottom line is that subconsciously, what will motivate an individual with ADHD lies in interest, curiosity, novelty, challenge, or urgency.[34]

Jennie Friedman

VII.

"Know science. No stigma."

~ Brain & Behavior Research Foundation

Jennie Friedman

ADHD IS A DIAGNOSIS, NOT A LABEL

Labels aren't always bad. It's how we, as humans, classify and connect with the world around us and with others. In a perfect world, people would just classify things or groups, like families, schools, churches but not people. Until that day comes though, I think understanding ADHD as a diagnosis is important. At school presentations, I've had parents tell me, "I just don't want my child labeled with ADHD," not realizing it's not a label it's a diagnosis.

I've also had adults at corporate workshops say, "I really don't want a disability label at work." I understand because the fear is that the individual with ADHD will be seen as *less than*. I always answer with this challenge though, "Is that worse than being labeled the other things?" *Other things* include a host of negative adjectives. Labels are a problem because it's the stigma that's the label. In my mind, the diagnosis of ADHD spits it all back in the faces of those who would use them. ADHD means:

Not broken, not bad, not wayward, not incorrigible, not defective, not hopeless, not dumb, not a failure, not lost, not a misfit, not an idiot, not lazy, not crazy, not a fool, not mental, not a hot mess, not ruined, not spoiled, not intentional, not cursed, not weird, not a freak, not stupid, not a screw up, not making it up, not naughty, not a product of bad parenting, not curable, not disobedient, not disturbed, not flawed...

ADHD means the person has a brain that works differently than someone without it. Their subconscious default system is different than the non-ADHD one, and they can't help the way they automatically react and move in the world without expending a lot of extra effort. It also can't be stressed enough that the stigma and shame of these labels are so seriously damaging; yet, people still don't get it. Would you honestly rather Johnny be labeled a bully, lazy, a troublemaker, or butthead than having ADHD? Not that ADHD is an excuse for bad behavior but at least we can know what we are dealing with and be more effective in helping him. Is Susie really better off regarded as a space cadet or a weirdo? What kinds of classmates will she turn off in childhood? What kinds of men will she turn on in adulthood?

When Johnny is wreaking havoc in the classroom because his ADHD is untreated, punishing him only works so much. Fast forward, Johnny has been continuously punished over the years and the other kids see this, they know. They go home and tell their parents how he chucked a spitball into Sally's hair and the teacher made him sit in the corner or sent him to the principal's office. How do you think Johnny's peers will regard him? Do you think he'll be invited over for play dates and parties? The even bigger question is how will Johnny regard Johnny?

There are so many ramifications for untreated ADHD even beyond low self-esteem. Someone with severe enough symptoms can have trouble keeping a job and relationships. People who talk excessively can have serious trouble being taken seriously. Many kids who get pushed through the school systems, because they are too much to handle can end up dropping out early compounding their difficulties in obtaining and sustaining employment. Did you know that the prison population is estimated to have 21 – 45% of inmates having ADHD?[35] The stigma around ADHD is a huge problem on so many levels, and not just for the people who have it but also for everyone. As a society it's time to get past the stupid stigma borne from ignorance. We know better so let's do better!

Neurodiversity

Neurodiversity is the concept of embracing the differences in the way each of our brains are wired. John Elder Robison, author of *Look Me in the Eye: My Life with Asperger's*, described it best, "neurodiversity is the idea that neurological differences like autism and ADHD are the result of normal, natural variation in the human genome."[36] Through the neurodiversity lens, ADHD, among other neurobiological conditions, does not become something that needs a cure. People with ADHD are not seen as broken or in need of fixing. Indeed, this idea is becoming increasingly supported by science where ADHD is considered only as some deviation from the standard in the range of cognitive differences.

Accepting these differences changes the whole conversation about them. Neurodiversity does not suggest that culturally inappropriate behaviors be accepted, but that the treatment of individuals with cognitive differences should include help and accommodations. Even these will be unique to individuals; there is no cookie-cutter solution for any issue. This is, in part, why I became an ADHD coach. Coaching addresses individuals uniquely so that they may figure out for themselves what solutions will work for them.

Feel Victimized or Live in Choice

I know some people can feel victimized by their loved ones behaviors, especially the behaviors that are due to an invisible disability like ADHD. Ultimately, it boils down to creating and sticking to boundaries, having open communication on both sides, and realizing that you can live in choice. You can choose to ignore the person and not have them in your life or you can choose creative interpretations and be more flexible. You can let them know of your expectations and disappointments. They have to return the favor. Together is the only way you move forward.

To leave it at this would be a huge disservice to the point of "Seeing in ADHD". The point is not just to understand why someone with ADHD acts the way they do. For one, it's not possible considering all the other factors that go into a person: beliefs, values, needs, as well as disposition and character, just to name a few. *No one is just his or her ADHD.* Plus, there is the likelihood of coexisting conditions. Just accepting that another's perception creates their perspective and that's just how it is would be passively tolerating what is sometimes bad behavior.

A loving, healthy relationship is co-created. When one person in the relationship has ADHD, an understanding of it is just the necessary foundation upon which to build. To see, understand, and know that your loved one with ADHD is normal is a foundational requirement of the relationship. It is through the ADHD lens you observe with your eyes then process it with your brain and finally choose how to look at and interpret what is happening in your relationship. You can become a part of the solution. Listen, acknowledge, and look for strategies that are built for the ADHD-brain.

My hope is that you have picked up some helpful knowledge that will bridge any distance that misunderstanding ADHD has created in your life. To leave feedback on this book, inquire about future books, or find out about the workshops associated with this book please visit: http://www.seeinadhd.com.

ABOUT THE AUTHOR

Jennie Friedman is an ADHD coach. She focuses on helping people who "suffer" from ADHD. Jennie created See in ADHD to help promote ADHD awareness and decrease the associated stigma. A professional ADHD coach, she specializes in helping people share their passions with the world. She puts her 20+ years of business development and marketing expertise to work in an ADHD-friendly way, expanding your opportunities for income and connectivity.

Jennie's family has wrestled with anxiety, depression, bipolar disorder, ADHD, and schizophrenia for generations. Growing up with her entire tribe affected sparked in her the drive to educate others how to embrace their differences so they can just focus on the most important business of loving one another.

Jennie Friedman

ENDNOTES

1.Dupar, L. (2013). More ways to succeed with ADHD (1st ed., ADHD Awareness Book Project). Granite Bay, CA: Coaching for ADHD. doi: 978-0615831640

2 Myths About ADHD. (2014, October). Retrieved February 9, 2015, from http://www.adhdawarenessmonth.org/old-stuff/myths-about-adhd/

3 ADHD Medications, an Overview. (2015). Retrieved February 9, 2015, from http://www.chadd.org/Understanding-ADHD/Parents-Caregivers-of-Children-with-ADHD/Evaluation-and-Treatment/ADHD-Medications-An-Overview.aspx

4 Power, T. J., PhD, & Soffer, S. L., PhD. (2014, March 21). Overview of ADHD: Principles of effective treatment. Lecture presented at Developmentally and Culturally Effective Psychosocial Interventions for Youth with ADHD in Pennsylvania, Philadelphia.

5 Symptoms and Diagnosis. (2014, September 29). Retrieved November 11, 2014, from http://www.cdc.gov/ncbddd/adhd/diagnosis.html

6 Whatshakin3. (2014, June 2). Dr. Russell Barkley ADHD is Not a Gift. Retrieved September 10, 2014, from http://www.youtube.com/watch?v=wSze0QPgbzU

7 About Dr. Brown. (n.d.). Retrieved February 7, 2015, from http://www.drthomasebrown.com/aboutdrbrown/

8 About Russell A. Barkley, Ph.D. (n.d.). Retrieved February 7, 2015, from http://www.russellbarkley.org/about.html

9 ABOUT US. (n.d.). Retrieved February 7, 2015, from http://www.dodsonadhdcenter.com/

10 The Brown Model of ADD/ADHD. (n.d.). Retrieved February 7, 2015, from http://www.drthomasebrown.com/add-adhd-model/

11 Dodson, W., MD. (n.d.). Secrets of the ADHD Brain. Retrieved October 22, 2014, from http://www.additudemag.com/adhd/article/10117.html

12 Executive Functioning. (n.d.). Retrieved February 7, 2015, from http://cogx.info/executive-functioning/

13 Dodson, W., MD. (n.d.). ADHD: Why We Do What We Do. Retrieved July 28, 2014, from http://www.additudemag.com/adhd/article/10497.html

14 Brown, T. E., MD. (2013). A new understanding of ADHD in children and adults: Executive function impairments. Routledge

15 Tivers, E. (2014, November 17). We are All Wired Differently! [Audio blog interview]. Retrieved from http://www.erictivers.com/#!ep-38/c8p8

16 Carter, D. (2014). Neural Networks - the Biological Location of Change. Retrieved February 10, 2015, from http://www.internet-of-the-

mind.com/neural_networks.html

17 Thomas, E. (2008). Understanding the Subconscious Mind. Retrieved October 22, 2014, from

http://www.effective-mind-control.com/understanding-the-subconscious-mind.html

18 Taylor, T. (n.d.). Brain. Retrieved October 22, 2014, from http://www.innerbody.com/image/nerv02.html

19 Dodson, W., MD. (2013, July). ADHD EXPERTS PODCAST EPISODE: Secrets of the ADHD Brain, Revealed [Audio blog interview]. Retrieved from http://www.additudemag.com/RCLP/thx/10300.html

20 Thomas, E. (2008). Understanding the Subconscious Mind. Retrieved October 22, 2014, from

http://www.effective-mind-control.com/understanding-the-subconscious-mind.html

21Dodson, W., MD. (n.d.). Secrets of the ADHD Brain. Retrieved October 22, 2014, from

http://www.additudemag.com/adhd/article/10117.html

22Kaur, A., & Kaur, S. (2012). About Spirit Voyage's 40 Day Global Sadhanas:. Retrieved November 18, 2014, from http%3A%2F%2Fwww.spiritvoyage.com%2Fglobalsadhana

23Dodson, W., MD. (n.d.). ADHD: Why We Do What We Do. Retrieved July 28, 2014, from

http://www.additudemag.com/adhd/article/10497.html

24 Brady, C., PhD, Hirschfeld, R. M., MD, & Barkley, R., PhD. (n.d.). Common Questions About ADHD... And Expert Answers! Retrieved October 22, 2014, from

http://www.additudemag.com/adhd/article/2509.html

25 Brown, T. E., MD. (2014). Smart but stuck: Emotions in teens and adults with ADHD (1st ed.). Jossey-Bass. doi: 111827928X

26 Blum, K., Chen, A. L.-C., Braverman, E. R., Comings, D. E., Chen, T. J., Arcuri, V., et al (2008). Attention-deficit-hyperactivity disorder and reward deficiency syndrome. Neuropsychiatric Disease and Treatment, 4(5), 893–918.

27 Dodson, W., MD. (n.d.). Secrets of the ADHD Brain. Retrieved October 22, 2014, from

http://www.additudemag.com/adhd/article/10117.html

28 Taylor, T. (n.d.). Brain. Retrieved October 22, 2014, from http://www.innerbody.com/image/nerv02.html

29 Taylor, T. (n.d.). Brain. Retrieved October 22, 2014, from http://www.innerbody.com/image/nerv02.html

30 Dodson, W., MD. (n.d.). Secrets of the ADHD Brain. Retrieved October 22, 2014, from

http://www.additudemag.com/adhd/article/10117.html

31 National Sleep Foundation. (2006). Sleep-Wake Cycle: Its Physiology and Impact on Health. Retrieved November 5, 2014, from http://sleepfoundation.org/sites/default/files/SleepWakeCycle.pdf

32 Drug Facts: Stimulant ADHD Medications: Methylphenidate and Amphetamines. (2014, January). Retrieved February 9, 2015, from http://www.drugabuse.gov/publications/drugfacts/stimulant-adhd-medications-methylphenidate-amphetamines

33 Matthews, M., Nigg, J. T., & Fair, D. A. (2014). Attention Deficit Hyperactivity Disorder. Current Topics in Behavioral Neurosciences, 16, 235–266. doi:10.1007/7854_2013_249

34 Duncan, D. (2014, August 26). Attention, Interest & Importance in ADHD [Audio blog post]. Retrieved from https://www.bcinterioradhdclinic.com/coach/adhdinsideout/understanding/interest-attention--focus.html

35 Quily, P. (2011). Up To 45% Of Prisoners Have ADHD Studies Show. Crime & Jail Are Costly, Treatment Is Cheap. adultaddstrengths.com/2011/01/12/adhd-and-crime-ignore-now-jail-later-15-clinical-studies/

36 Robison, J. E. (2007). Look me in the eye: My life with Asperger's. New York: Crown.

DISCLAIMER

Made in the USA
Columbia, SC
21 December 2018